The Repurposed & Upcycled Life

A Women's Small Group Bible Study

Michelle Rayburn

FAITH CREATIVITY LIFE BOOKS

Contents

Contents

Introduction

This study is a companion to *The Repurposed and Upcycled Life*. The intent is to help you go a little deeper into what the Bible says about the topics covered in the book. This Bible study resource expands the "Getting Personal" section at the end of each book chapter to help small groups work through each topic together. You'll find some of the content from that section included here, edited to fit a small group setting.

This not intended to be an exhaustive study of scripture. It is not a Bible study that requires any pre-knowledge of the Bible. It is an opportunity for friends, neighbors, and book club members to converse about the truth found in the Bible and to figure out how it applies to real life.

Some will meet in living rooms, others at a church, and still others may gather at a coffee shop. Yum! The idea is that women gather. This connection offers an opportunity to learn, discover, and grow together.

No Pressure
Give your fellow members permission to ask questions or share thoughts, without judgment. All women should feel valued and validated as they discuss. There may be times you need to agree to disagree and that's okay! Make this a safe place where you keep anything shared in the group confidential.

It's helpful if one member of the group facilitates moving the discussion ahead to the next question, but there is no preparation needed ahead of time. There is also no homework necessary, outside of reading one chapter of *The Repurposed and Upcycled Life* during the week. All other suggestions for outside activities are optional. That's great news for busy women!

The study has 15 weeks, one for each chapter of the book. Only have 10 weeks? No problem! You can combine weeks, or omit topics that you prefer to skip, to make it fit your needs.

Your time of prayer should fit your group and your style. Some groups are comfortable with every member taking turns praying out loud. Others aren't as comfortable, and prefer to have one person pray for everyone. Some will break into smaller groups. Get to know each other and find something that is most comfortable for you.

Supplies Needed

- In addition to this study guide, each group member will need a copy of *The Repurposed and Upcycled Life.**

- A Bible. Any translation. Smart phones and tablets welcome.

- A pen.

- A notebook (optional). This may be helpful for journaling exercises, or for writing down what doesn't fit on the worksheets. Or you may like the journaling pages scattered throughout this book.

- Colored pencils or fine-tipped markers for those who would like to color in doodles.

Leader Tips

If you're the group facilitator and would like additional tips for group discussion and leadership helps, see the section for leaders at the end of the book.

Ready?

That's it! You're ready to discover *your* repurposed and upcycled life.

*Discounts on group orders of *The Repurposed and Upcycled Life* available at www.michellerayburn.com.

Week One: Junk in the Trunk
Unloading Emotional Baggage

Preparation

If you haven't already done it, please read the introduction ("From Michelle's Heart to Yours") and chapter 1 of *The Repurposed and Upcycled Life.*

Warm Up

- Is there something about the concept of "junk in the trunk" that resonated with you as you read the chapter?

- How has emotional baggage hindered you or held you back in life? How has it affected you in your family relationships, or work?

- Michelle admitted to photoshopping family pictures, standing in the back row for pictures, and stuffing herself into shapewear. What things have you done that show your discomfort with your body shape?

Explore the Bible

Let's take a look at some snapshots from the Bible that show us something about the burdens we might carry around as junk packed away in our emotional trunk. Look up these verses and have someone in the group read them aloud. Use the questions below for a discussion springboard.

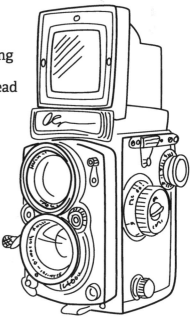

Guilt - Psalm 38:4

- In what way might guilt become baggage for us?

Shame - Psalm 25:3

- What good news does this verse contain about shame?

Rules and Legalism - Matthew 11:28-30

Jesus made this statement in reference to how following him compared to getting bogged down in rules and legalism that some church leaders in his day wanted to pile on people.

- In what way can some church regulations feel like a burden to some people? [Examples: being good, no dancing, no drinking, certain styles of clothing, rules about food, etc.]

- What is it about Jesus' offer that **you think** makes his burden seem lighter? [Hint: Jesus offers salvation without us having to earn it}

Worries and Cares - Psalm 55:22

- What does this verse tell us will happen when we give our worries to God?

Sin and Other Hindrances - Hebrews 12:1-2

These verses compare life to running a race. Have you ever seen a runner compete with thick layers of clothing and lugging a suitcase in each hand?

- Discuss what it means to throw off what hinders.

- Talk about what might be in the "trunk" some women lug around and how it affects them. Examples: guilt, negative thoughts, anger, bitterness, labels, fear, self-doubt, insecurity, abuse, hatred, abandonment, unforgiveness.

- What does the passage mean when it talks about the sin that so easily entangles?

- Read 1 John 1:9 to see what happens when we "throw off" or confess our sin to God.

Letting Go of Baggage

- What is one word you would use to describe how you feel about your baggage?

Maybe "free" was your word. If so, that's great! If not, imagine how it might feel to be emotionally free from past hurts. It might be tempting to ignore it and stuff it down. But God wants us to live free of that hindrance. He has a plan for your life, a plan that includes using your pain for his glory.

Read Paul's words from **1 Timothy 1:12-17** aloud together.

Now take a moment for each of you to read it to yourself below. Put your name in the first blank. Then fill in the other blank with something that describes you before God made a change in you:

> I thank Christ Jesus our Lord, who has given me strength, that he considered me faithful, appointing me to his service. Even though I, _____ , was once _____, I was shown mercy because I acted in ignorance and unbelief. The grace of our Lord was poured out on me abundantly, along with the faith and love that are in Christ Jesus. Here is a trustworthy saying that deserves full acceptance: Christ Jesus came into the world to save sinners—of whom I am the worst. But for that very reason I was shown mercy so that in me, the worst of sinners, Christ Jesus might display his unlimited patience as an example for those who would believe on him and receive eternal life. Now to the King eternal, immortal, invisible, the only God, be honor and glory forever and ever. Amen.

- Paul talks about God displaying his patience in him as an example for others. What might God be able to display, or show others, in you as a result of what you have been through?

Prayer

Focus on thanking God for how he relieves us of our baggage. Praise him for the way he shows mercy when we don't deserve it.

At-Home Action

- Journal about how fully accepting God's grace could change, or how it has already changed, your life. Use the journaling pages scattered throughout this workbook if you'd like.

- Create a visual reminder of how much God loves you and lavishes his grace on you by making a bead bracelet from inexpensive alphabet beads, colored plastic beads, and elastic string. Spell out the word or words you most need to hear. Examples: He Loves Me, Grace, Be Real, Forgiven. Wear that bracelet as a visual reminder of what God has done and is doing in you.

Journaling Page

Journaling Page

Journaling Page

_____

_____

_____

_____

_____

_____

_____

_____

_____

_____

_____

_____

_____

_____

_____

_____

_____

_____

_____

_____

_____

_____

_____

_____

_____

_____

_____

_____

_____

_____

_____

_____

_____

Week Two: Dust Bunnies and Bad ~~Hare~~ Hair Days

Letting Go of Pride and Perfection

Preparation

Please read chapter 2 of *The Repurposed and Upcycled Life*.

Warm Up

Choose one of the following statements that applies to you and share it with the group.

- My coworkers, family members, or roommates have commented on my perfectionism.
- I cannot stand to leave any dishes in the sink, clutter on the kitchen counter, or laundry unfolded without it bothering me very much.
- I can't have friends over until I mop the floor and clean away all of the clutter.
- When I sew or do crafts, I rip out seams multiple times until the project is perfect, or I re-do projects until I get it right.
- I have trouble finishing things I start.
- I am critical of the people around me, and I am very particular about how I do things.
- None of these statements describe me. I'm as laid back as they come.
- All of the above statements describe me. Please be nice to me.

If you are not a perfectionist, perhaps you know and love someone who is. We might all recognize a few traits in ourselves, but we can function pretty well, despite a few perfectionist tendencies.

If someone close to you is a perfectionist, it might be difficult to know how to love him or her. As you do the study this week, watch for ways you might be able to be an encouragement to a perfectionist.

Explore the Bible

Read Matthew 5:48.

- What do you think it means to be perfect here? [Hint: God is complete and without sin or error]

We might be tempted to use a verse like that one to put a lot of pressure on ourselves. But that verse isn't about being perfect in the way we might think of it. God loves, and then he encourages us to be like God the Father. He sets the standards for loving others high, however, God doesn't expect perfection through our own efforts. Whew! Right?

Be encouraged by these words. "His divine power has given us everything we need for life and godliness through our knowledge of him who called us by his own glory and goodness" (2 Peter 1:3).

Read Luke 18:9-14.

Michelle talked in chapter 2 about how she realized how much like the Pharisee she once was, and how God worked on her attitudes.

- According to verse 9, why did Jesus tell this parable?

- What was wrong with the prayer of the Pharisee?

- What made the prayer of the tax collector different?

- In verse 14, some translations talk about the contrast between being humble, and exalting ourselves. What is another way of describing "exalting ourselves?"

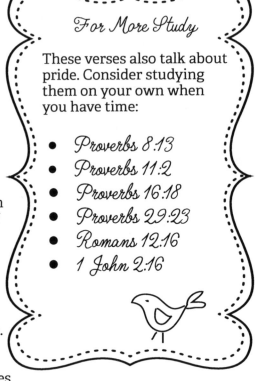

For More Study

These verses also talk about pride. Consider studying them on your own when you have time:

- *Proverbs 8:13*
- *Proverbs 11:2*
- *Proverbs 16:18*
- *Proverbs 29:23*
- *Romans 12:16*
- *1 John 2:16*

The problem with perfectionism is it often comes along with a strong sense of pride. It isn't something we like to confront in ourselves, but it gets in the way of connecting with other people.

When we work so hard to follow the rules and live by our self-made standard of perfection, we can sometimes pat ourselves on the back for the outcome of our efforts.

It's tough to hear, but that attitude isn't the attitude of Christ. Confronting perfectionism also involves confronting pride. [Please note: finding joy in our work and admiring the outcome is not the same as being prideful. Pride says, "I'm better than other people."]

Discuss

- How can a person know the difference between taking pride in the excellence of work, and the haughty pride the Bible warns us to watch out for?

Read 2 Corinthians 12:9.

- What does this say about perfection?

- How can this verse encourage those trying to achieve perfection in their own efforts?

Read 2 Corinthians 12:10.

- How is it that Paul can say here that he is the strongest when he is weak?

- Think of a time when you felt helpless on your own and you felt God take over the situation. Briefly describe it for the group, and explain how it felt to be helpless and strong at the same time.

There is no character flaw that cannot be transformed by the power of God. When we invite him to change us, he does. The Apostle Paul, who wrote the verses we just looked at in 2nd Corinthians, is an example of God's transformation.

Paul was a Pharisee, misguided by his zeal to follow rules and traditions to the point where he would kill Christians. But when God turned around Paul's thinking through an encounter we will study in Week 6, the change was radical.

People were astonished by the change when Paul began to preach the message of Jesus–the opposite of what he once stood for. God can bring about a radical change in us too!

Overcoming Perfectionism

Sometimes it is difficult to be vulnerable enough to admit our struggles to friends. It's easy to laugh about our perfectionism with friends, but it takes courage to admit the habit is rooted in pride.

- What action step do you think God would want you to take to work on your perfectionism and/or pride? What do you think will be the hardest part about taking that step?

- If you feel comfortable, admit your weakness to the group, and ask for prayer for God's transformation.

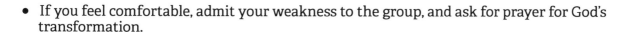

Prayer

As you pray, focus on appreciating God's perfection and ask for his help in cultivating a humble nature in us. Praise him for the promise in 2 Corinthians 12:9 that his power is perfect in our weakness.

At-Home Action

Think of someone in your life who isn't perfect, yet whom you love despite his or her flaws. Or think of something you own that you love despite its imperfections. Maybe it's an heirloom, a worn quilt, or a piece of furniture you rescued from the curb.

- Take a picture of that person or object and print it out or use it as your computer screen saver. Each time you look at the photo, remind yourself how much God loves you despite your imperfections, too.

- Journal about your own struggle with pride and perfectionism. If comfortable, also share with a trusted friend who will help to hold you accountable to letting God work on that quality in you.

Journaling Page

Journaling Page

Journaling Page

_____

_____

_____

_____

_____

_____

_____

_____

_____

_____

_____

_____

_____

_____

_____

_____

_____

_____

_____

_____

_____

_____

_____

_____

_____

_____

_____

Week Three: Better Homes and Varmints

Protecting Your Spiritual Identity

Preparation

Please read chapter 3 of *The Repurposed and Upcycled Life.*

Warm Up

As you begin this week, choose one or two of these points to discuss:

- What not-so-perfect traditions are part of your holiday activities and preparations?

- Think of a time when you had the perfect party or event planned and something ruined it. Share in one or two sentences how you felt when your perfect plans fell apart.

- Have you ever made a resolution to change something about yourself? Perhaps to get in shape, eat healthier, change a habit or overcome an attitude problem. Did you stick with it? What happened if you didn't stick with it? How do you respond when you feel like you have failed at something?

Explore the Bible

In the last session, we talked about the story of Paul and how he was changed after he began to follow Jesus. Sometimes, we mistakenly assume that following Christ means we will never struggle with our old behaviors again. So, when temptation with old attitudes and actions does come up, it can become a dangerous tipping point where we give up and go back to our old character. We can find hope once again in Paul's story. This man who followed God had his share of struggle, but he didn't give up.

Read Romans 7:15-24 to learn more out about Paul's struggle.

Discuss

- What does Paul decide his real problem is?

- Share about a time when you asked yourself, "What is my problem?" What emotion or feeling was connected with your experience?

Was there ever a time in your past, or present, where you learned that following the rules was the ultimate goal? There is a term for when we're centered more on the rules than we are on the motive for following the rules. It's called legalism. It's when we base everything on our own effort to be good. It results in a "try harder" mentality.

Although it might sound like Paul is making excuses when he talks about his efforts, he isn't. Paul doesn't rest on good intentions. He genuinely wants to get to a solution. Let's continue reading to see what solution Paul offers.

Read Romans 7:25-8:11

- What is Paul's solution to the struggle to get rid of the behavior that doesn't please God?

Ah, the Sunday school answer to all questions. If you haven't been to Sunday school, that's ok. For those raised in the church culture, there is a joke that the correct answer to all questions is "Jesus."

Yes. Jesus is the answer. But let's explore *why* he is the answer. In those first few verses of Romans 8, we learn that following the rules by itself is not the way to overcome our old behavior.

Rules provide us a moral and ethical guide, but following them perfectly is not the path to freedom. Rules and legalism are the path to bondage. In Romans, Paul shows us that it is God's power in us that sets us free from this bondage.

> **Romans 8:12, 14-15**
>
> "Therefore, dear brothers and sisters, you have no obligation to do what your sinful nature urges you to do... For all who are led by the Spirit of God are children of God. So you have not received a spirit that makes you fearful slaves. Instead, you received God's Spirit when he adopted you as his own children."

Read the excerpt at the right from Romans 8.

- What is it about our relationship with God that makes following him different from following a list of rules?

- Consider the relationship between earthly parents and children. What is different in parents who focus on a relationship with their children more than on the rules of the household?

- As you think about the previous question, what is different about focusing on our relationship with God and on the power given to us by the Holy Spirit more than on following God's rules?

Consider these words:

"Since we believe that Christ died for all, we also believe that we have all died to our old life. He died for everyone so that those who receive his new life will no longer live for themselves. Instead, they will live for Christ, who died and was raised for them. So we have stopped evaluating others from a human point of view. At one time we thought of Christ merely from a human point of view. How differently we know him now! This means that anyone who belongs to Christ has become a new person. The old life is gone; a new life has begun!" (2 Corinthians 5:14-17)

- What does it mean to belong to Christ? How is that different from knowing about him and going to church?

- Describe what becoming a new person means for you personally.

If you have time, break into pairs and tell each other a short version of who you were before you knew Christ and how you have changed now.

Since Jesus was the only perfect person, we know we will mess up sometimes. However, God gives us his power through his Holy Spirit, as adopted children, to have victory over the power of evil. Sin and former behaviors no longer define you!

Perhaps you also need a reminder that making mistakes does not lead to God's rejection. He loves you, wherever you are on your journey. We will explore that idea more in the next lesson, as well.

Prayer

As you pray together, consider how you might seek the power of the Holy Spirit in relation to your needs. Let your tone be one of declaring the victory Jesus has over sin, and claim that victory as family of the one who has defeated Satan's power.

At-Home Action

- Start a Pinterest board that shows before and after projects. As you search for ideas, consider how although the object has a similar shape to its former condition, it no longer looks the same. Remember, Jesus takes our imperfections and our best qualities and remakes us into someone who shows his glory in the "after" picture.

- Soul-searching: Is there something in your life that keeps pulling you back toward your old behavior rather than drawing you to Christ? One of the most difficult action steps to take is letting go of something that is part of our old identity. What step will you take to move away from that setting or situation?

Verses for additional personal study

1 Peter 2:9, John 1:12

1 John 5:18-20, Galatians 3:26-27

Psalm 32, John 15:15

Journaling Page

Journaling Page

_____

_____

_____

_____

_____

_____

_____

_____

_____

_____

_____

_____

_____

_____

_____

_____

_____

_____

_____

_____

_____

_____

_____

_____

Week Four: Objects in the Mirror Are Closer Than They Appear
Letting Go of the Past and Living in the Present

Preparation

Please read chapter 4 of *The Repurposed and Upcycled Life.*

Warm Up

- What is one of your happiest memories you can recall?

- Do you think you spend more time looking back or looking forward? If you look back, is it because you wish you could change things or because life was better then? Do you love to reminisce? If you prefer to look to the future, what would you say you are most focused on?

Explore the Bible

Do you remember playing games with friends as a child when you'd declare a do-over because of a tie? Inevitably, there would be someone in the group who wanted a do-over simply because he or she didn't like the outcome of the play. Wouldn't it be nice if life had a built in rule that allowed us to undo our mistakes?

In Chapter 4 of *The Repurposed and Upcycled Life,* Michelle gave four steps that helped her move forward without being hindered by regret and wishing for a do-over. As we explore the Bible, we will follow those four steps to be FREE of living stuck in the past.

F - *Forgive Others*

Let's explore the model we can use for forgiving others that we find in the Bible. It isn't likely that some of the people who have deeply hurt you will come to a place of realizing the pain they have caused and ask you for forgiveness. Yet, if you don't forgive, it can stand in the way of your own healing. Jesus gave us an example to follow.

Read Luke 23:32-39.

This story is part of Jesus' crucifixion. Notice that none of the people who insulted or mocked him asked for forgiveness. In fact, they just kept going with it. Yet, Jesus said, "Father, forgive them, for they don't know what they are doing."

Discuss

- Why do you think it mattered to Jesus to forgive them if they weren't sorry for their actions?

Before he was on the cross, Jesus had instructed his disciples in what is called the Sermon on the Mount that they should not pray to God for forgiveness and expect to receive it if they had not first forgiven others (Mark 11:25). In other words, unforgiveness can be a hindrance to our own spiritual growth. He doesn't mention anything about the other person deserving forgiveness.

- What do you think is the most difficult part of forgiving someone who doesn't deserve it?

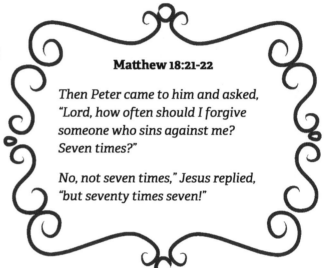

Matthew 18:21-22

Then Peter came to him and asked, "Lord, how often should I forgive someone who sins against me? Seven times?"

No, not seven times," Jesus replied, "but seventy times seven!"

Forgiving doesn't necessarily mean letting someone off the hook for their actions. But it does mean letting yourself free of the bondage of anger, hatred and resentment that hinders you from fully loving the people in your life.

- Read the passage from Matthew at the right and then talk about why this concept is relevant in our lives in light of how our culture views forgiveness.

- Why is it difficult to forgive someone for the same offense more than once?

R - *Receive Grace*

Sometimes, as we look back, it isn't others that need forgiving, it's ourselves. Some of you have no problem freely offering forgiveness to those who have wronged you, but you can't let go of clubbing **yourself for something that happened long ago.** Little circumstances can trigger a big reaction, and you either withdraw into self-loathing, or you lash out in reactive anger.

We peeked at this verse in another study, but let's look at it again.

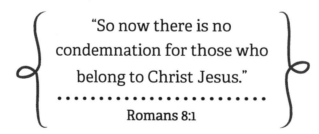

"So now there is no condemnation for those who belong to Christ Jesus."
. . . .
Romans 8:1

Discuss and define the following terms from the verse, using a dictionary if you need further insight:

- *now*
- *no condemnation*
- *who belong*

- In light of this verse, what is the truth about God's grace and our failures? Why do you think it is sometimes hard to accept this truth?

When a guilty criminal receives a pardon, all charges are canceled. Even better, this means that a criminal record ceases to exist, and background checks come back with the result "no criminal record found."

When we confess sin to God and ask for forgiveness, he pardons us by accepting the penalty payment of Jesus Christ in our place. Record canceled. Slate clean.

Imagine how it must feel to a prisoner to receive the news that he or she has been pardoned, to have shackles removed and to walk out of the prison gates. Imagine the freedom!

That freedom is yours in Christ. You are no longer shackled to your past. No longer charged with your mistakes.

Read Micah 7:18-19.

This passage from the Old Testament speaks to God's people, Israel, and yet it still applies to how God pardons us today.

- Some translations say he delights in showing mercy, and others refer to delighting in showing unfailing love. What does it mean for you, when you consider that he "delights" showing love?

- What is the significance of throwing our sins into the depths of the ocean? (This is a subjective response for you to consider the meaning, and there is no right or wrong answer.)

E - *Engage in the Present*

Have you considered how everything you've been through is part of your story? It's part of what brought you to this place. But if you're looking back, you might miss the opportunities God has put right in front of you.

As you pedal a bike forward, your eyes would logically look ahead, rather than over your shoulder. Obviously, right? Sometimes it isn't obvious in life. And then we wonder why we end up figuratively crashing and burning again and again.

Where are your eyes?

Read Philippians 3:8-14.

As you wrap up your session think about how having a future in heaven changes how you live on earth.

- When you look ahead with a focus on Jesus Christ, what are some practical ways you can point others toward a relationship with Jesus as a result of what you have been through?

- In what ways are you more equipped to minister to others because of your freedom from guilt and shame?

Prayer

Would you pray for one another? Be open in asking for prayer related to a specific aspect of the path to being FREE: forgiving others, receiving grace, eliminating guilt, embracing the present. If some are uncomfortable with praying aloud, that's okay. No one will force you. However, would you consider stepping out of your comfort zone to say a single sentence on behalf of a sister in the room? It could be a simple as, "Lord, please help Julie to forgive the person who hurt her so deeply." Or, "Please help Beth accept how much you love her."

At-Home Action

- For various reasons, we can't always talk to or write to the person we need to forgive. For the sake of your own closure, it might be helpful to write out a letter of forgiveness, anyway. Perhaps you'll destroy it when you're finished, or you might tuck it in your Bible as a reminder of your freedom.

- This week's subject can be a heavy one. Sometimes in realizing how we need to forgive someone, we also realize how we have hurt someone else as a result of our pain. Pray about how you might approach someone to ask for their forgiveness for your actions.

  Hints: Avoid phrases such as "if I hurt you" and directly address your action. "It must have hurt you very much when I did _____. I was so wrong to say/do that to you. I apologize for my actions and I ask you to forgive me. I know it won't make up for what I did, but I'd like to begin with this apology."

Journaling Page

Journaling Page

Week Five: Silver Hairs, Chin Fuzz & Fringe Benefits
Getting Perspective Aligned

Preparation

Please read chapter 5 of *The Repurposed and Upcycled Life.*

Warm Up

- On a scale of 1-10, with 10 being very stressful and 1 being not stressful, how stressed do you feel about getting older?

- What parts of aging bother you the most? (Wrinkles, aching joints, gray hair, waistline changes, health changes, memory problems...did you really need depressing examples to carry out this discussion?)

- What parts of aging have you laughed off and enjoyed?

Explore the Bible

There are a lot of things that we purchase in this life that aren't going to withstand through our lifetime. How many toasters have you tossed? Or vacuum cleaners. Or televisions. Or irons. Oh, wait–those might last longer, if you've sworn off ironing unless you have to.

Now, consider what God says about his dependability.

Read Isaiah 46:3-10.

Let's camp here for a little while and look at what this passage says. We will come back to the first verses in a few minutes. In the meantime, let's look at what the people were doing that prompted God's words to them. Read verse 6-7 again.

You probably haven't created a cast gold or silver idol lately, but that's what these people were doing.

- However, before we judge, can you name some activities and possessions we pour our money into hoping it will make us happy?

Let's backtrack to the first few verses we read.

- Read verse 4 again. All the way to old age, he will carry and sustain us. Let that soak in for a moment and see if anyone can think of anything else in life that comes with that kind of a lifetime guarantee.

Discuss

This passage from Isaiah reminds us that God is with us from the cradle to the grave and there is nothing the compares to him.

- Talk about some of the aspects of everyday life that make it difficult to keep the right perspective when hard times come.

In chapter 5 of *The Repurposed and Upcycled Life*, you read a synopsis of the life of Joseph from the Bible. Joseph's whole story covers 13 chapters from Genesis 37 to Genesis 50. If you have time on your own, read the story and look for the ways where God turns Joseph's trash into treasure.

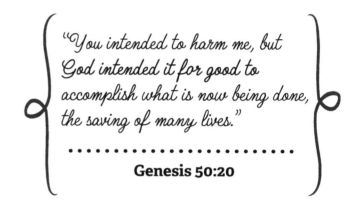

"You intended to harm me, but God intended it for good to accomplish what is now being done, the saving of many lives."

Genesis 50:20

In the meantime, let's look at a few high points of what made it possible for Joseph to have such a positive perspective on all of the junk he went through.

Read Genesis 39:2-6.

- What is the key to Joseph's success? Why is this significant?

Shortly after this part of the story, trouble came and Joseph was unjustly put in prison. Read Genesis 39:20-23.

- Again, what pattern do you see, even in the middle of this struggle?

Two years passed before Joseph had an opportunity to show God's power through interpreting the dream of Pharaoh and he was taken out of prison. He rose in power, appointed by Pharaoh to be second in command in Egypt.

Read Genesis 41:50-52.

- What is Joseph's perspective on what he has been through, when we see what he named his sons?

Some time later, after being reunited with his brothers, they feared he would retaliate for what they had done more than 15 years earlier.

- Read Joseph's response in Genesis 45:4-8a when he revealed his identity to his brothers. What do you think it took for him to get to a place where he thought this way about what they had put him through?

- If you have thoughts similar to Joseph's about something difficult from your own life, would you be willing to share briefly with the group about the process of shifting your perspective about it?

Joseph's actions and words show that he forgave his brothers and that he didn't become bitter about the fallout caused by their actions.

Whether your frustration is about growing older, job stress, a difficult spouse or wounds caused long ago by someone with malicious intent, you have an opportunity to change your perspective on your situation.

God is with you, just as he was with Joseph.

Prayer

In your prayer time, pray specifically for attitudes that honor God. It's easy to ask God to fix a situation and make it work out the way we would hope, but it's more difficult to ask him to fix our attitudes about the situation. Pray that God would soften hard edges and break down walls related to any damage done by bitterness.

At-Home Action

- Sometimes, the best way to see our way out of the darkness of our own difficulty is to serve somewhere to help others who are experiencing even more difficulty. Look for a place in your community where you can serve women in need. Perhaps it is a women's shelter, or it's a food pantry, a local pregnancy crisis center, or a hospital.

- Consider doing the above as a group activity.

- Journal about how your experiences, good or bad, have deepened your faith and helped you to trust God's truth more. Write about how a Joseph approach to your trials and disappointments could be something God can use as a positive influence on someone else.

Journaling Page

_____
_____
_____
_____
_____
_____
_____
_____
_____
_____
_____
_____
_____
_____
_____
_____
_____
_____
_____
_____
_____
_____

Journaling Page

_____
_____
_____
_____
_____
_____
_____
_____
_____
_____
_____
_____
_____
_____
_____
_____
_____
_____
_____
_____
_____
_____
_____
_____
_____
_____
_____

Journaling Page

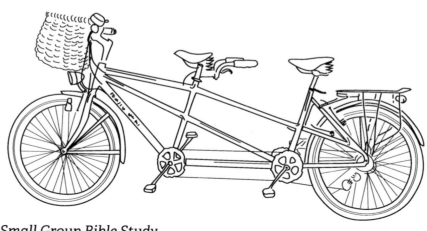

Week Six: From Trash to Treasure
Discovering Beauty in the Junk

Preparation

Please read chapter 6 of *The Repurposed and Upcycled Life.*

Optional: Have "Hello My Name Is" nametags and pens available for later in this lesson.

Warm Up

- What is the best item you have ever rescued from the trash? Was it a piece of furniture, an article of clothing, a picture or possibly something you repurposed into something else?

- What was it that made you want to put it to use?

Explore the Bible

Many of us love before-and-after stories. It's the success behind many DIY television shows about flipping old houses, transforming flea market finds and souping up junky cars into desirable collectibles. In order for the transformation to happen, someone must see the potential and have a vision for what it could be. What looks like a hopeless case or impossibility to everyone else isn't impossible in the eyes of the one to does the transforming.

Today, we're going to look at the life of the Apostle Paul (his Roman name), who was also known as Saul (his Hebrew name)–a hopeless cause in the eyes of some who may have known him before God got a hold on him. His change may have seemed like an impossibility in the eyes of some skeptics who met him after it took place.

Why would it seem impossible? Because Saul was the furthest thing from a Christ-follower he could be!

Read Paul's story in Acts 9:1-31.

This is a long passage, but Paul's transformation is a powerful demonstration of what our God can do!

Discuss

- What does the disciple named Ananias call Saul in verse 17? Why is this significant?

- Notice in verse 20, Saul began to preach at once that Jesus was the Son of God. Why did this startle so many people?

- How do you think you might have reacted if you had been one of the Jews living in Damascus?

Let's fast forward a bit to after Saul (Paul) is traveling and preaching.

Read 1 Timothy 1:12-17.

- What does Paul call himself in verse 13?

God poured out what Paul calls abundant grace on him and Paul transformed from a hater of Christians to one who followed Christ.

- In verse 15 of the passage you just read, Paul described himself as the worst of sinners. According to verse 16, what was God's purpose for using Paul instead of someone else for this task?

- Look back at verse 12 again. What three things did God do for which Paul is thankful?

God performs radical makeovers in people who others might consider hopeless causes. Why? One reason is given in verse 16, which we just discussed:

"...as an example for those who would believe in him and receive eternal life."

- How do you feel about the idea that your struggle and God's alteration of your heart might be so that someone else can see an example of God's patience and power?

It's important to note that in 1 Timothy, when Paul is talking about himself, especially in verse 13, he says, "I was once," not "I am." He was once a blasphemer and a persecutor and a violent man. He does not wear those labels anymore.

When God changes us, sometimes we forget that he gives us new labels to wear. We are not tied to those old labels anymore. Yes, we bear scars of things we have been through, but those scars are evidence of healing, not labels that condemn us.

Take a few minutes to complete the activity in the boxes below. List some of the old labels about yourself that you still wear. Then list the truth about who you are in Christ. See the list of examples below if you need help.

Labels I don't want to wear: Unwanted, Divorced, Frumpy, Abused, Stupid, Ugly, Loser, Worthless, Lazy, Angry, Bitter, Ashamed, Rejected, Afraid, Addicted, Victim, Hopeless, Broken.

Labels Christ gives to me: Conqueror, Forgiven, Child of God, Loved, Free, Blessed, Friend of God, Accepted, Hopeful, Alive with Christ, Temple of God, New Creation, Bold, Redeemed, Belonging, Complete, Significant.

Old labels I still wear: *Who I really am in Christ:*

- Looking at the labels on your list, which part of who you are in Christ is the most difficult for you to accept?

- Have each person in your group complete this statement and then say it out loud:

Hello, I used to wear the label of _____(worthless, insecure, angry, etc.),

but in Christ I am now _____(loved, accepted, forgiven, etc.).

- If you have "Hello My Name Is" labels available, have each person write a word about their new name in Christ on the label and challenge each other to wear it for the rest of the day.

In Galatians 2:20, Paul says, "My old self has been crucified with Christ. It is no longer I who live, but Christ lives in me. So I live in this earthly body by trusting in the Son of God, who loved me and gave himself for me."

Prayer

As you pray together, remember that Jesus, the Son of God, loves you and gave himself for you so that his qualities and character can live in you. Hold hands, or place your hands on the shoulders of the women sitting on either side of you as you pray. Take turns praying for each other, using the labels we wear in Christ as you pray for each person by name.

At-Home Action

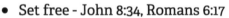

Continue to study what the Bible says about who you are:

- Set free - John 8:34, Romans 6:17
- Redeemed - Isaiah 43:1
- Restored - Ezekiel 36:24, Joel 2:32
- Ransomed - Ephesians 1:7, I Peter 1:19, Revelation 5:9, Mark 10:45, Hebrews 9:15, 1 Timothy 2:6
- Forgiven - Ephesians 1:7-8, Colossians 1:1,
- Adopted / Child of God - Ephesians 1:5, John 1:12, I John 3:1, Galatians 3:26
- Friend of God - John 15:15
- Blessed - Ephesians 1:3
- Made for a Purpose - Ephesians 2:10

Journaling Page

Journaling Page

_____
_____
_____
_____
_____
_____
_____
_____
_____
_____
_____
_____
_____
_____
_____
_____
_____

_____
_____
_____
_____
_____
_____
_____

Week Seven: Tooth Fairy Decay
Making Peace with Guilt and Regret

Preparation

Please read chapter 7 of *The Repurposed and Upcycled Life*.

Supplies: Small piece of paper or a sticky note for each woman

Warm Up

- Could you relate to the tooth fairy faux pas in chapter 7? If so, share your own story from either your childhood or your parenting moments.

- If you could have a do-over as a friend, a wife, or a mother, what would you change? What haunts you that you wish you could erase?

As women, we typically have strong opinions about what is right for our family: work outside of the home or stay home, home school or public school, television or no television, sugar or no sweets. The problem comes when we attempt to impose our choice on others, as though ours was the only right point of view.

We also have the potential to fall into shaming other women. If you've ever felt as if you didn't measure up to other women, raise your hand. If you've ever felt as if you needed to hide your struggle from other women, raise your hand. You aren't alone.

Explore the Bible

Too often, we forget God is all about redemption, about starting over as if our past never happened. We might hold on to our own regret or we might claim some sinister pleasure in reminding others of their past shame. Whatever the case may be, it is important to remind ourselves that Jesus came to set people free, not to hold them in bondage to pain, guilt or regret.

Read John 4:1-30, 39-42.

The Samaritan woman, whose name we never learn in the story, came to the well to draw water in the middle of the day. It was the custom in that time to draw water at the end of the day, when it was cooler (see Genesis 24:11 for a reference).

Discuss

- Based on her conversation with Jesus, why do you think she was there in the middle of the day?

The Samaritans practiced a religion that was a mixture of Judaism and idolatry (2 Kings 17:26-28) and there was a separation, even sometimes hatred, between the Jews and the Samaritans . They were also not seen favorably by Jewish leaders (John 8:48). This woman implied in John 4:9 that Jesus would be seen as unclean by associating with her.

- What does it tell us about Jesus that he intentionally traveled to this region and that he spoke to this woman?

- What was his tone in his conversation with her?

Notice Jesus didn't pretend to endorse this woman's choices, but he didn't condemn her either. He was matter-of-fact about her situation and he explained the solution – eternal life.

Think of a time when someone brought up or shared something that embarrassed you. Maybe it was a photo at a family reunion slide show. Maybe it was a video someone shared on social media. Perhaps your older sister told a story about you that you would rather forget.

- Share with the group how you felt about being reminded of something you would rather forget or having your secrets exposed in front of someone else.

The woman in the story didn't seem put out by the fact that Jesus knew so much about her. **Review verses 25-26 and 39-42 again.**

- Imagine what it was like for this woman to hear Jesus claim to be the Messiah she had just mentioned. Why do you think she was excited rather than ashamed that Jesus knew about about her past?

- What was the ultimate result of her testimony?

God Uses Imperfect People

God uses imperfect people to accomplish his purposes! This is great news. Before she had a chance to go home and get her life on a new track, her testimony was already bringing people to Jesus. It is important for us to remember that God can use us to make a difference for someone else, no matter where we are in our journey.

But we have to let go of guilt and regret and move forward. Shame is like strings that tether us to our past and keep us enslaved to fear. Let's discover how to cut the strings.

Read Psalm 103:8-14. There are five reminders here that can help cut the ties to guilt and regret:

1. God is compassionate and full of love.
2. God does not give us what we deserve for our sins.
3. God removes our past sins in a way too big to describe other than, forever gone.
4. God adopts us as his children.
5. God remembers we are human.

Mercy and Grace

Mercy is not getting what I deserve. Grace is getting something I don't deserve. God offers both mercy and grace.

- What is different about you since accepting the idea that God doesn't keep punishing us for our past mistakes (mercy) and that he gives us the gift of eternal life without us having to earn it (grace)?

- In John 4:14, Jesus tells the Samaritan woman about a well of eternal life that bubbles up. What kind of a picture does the phrase "a fresh bubbling spring" create for you about Jesus' love and mercy?

- Which of the five truths from Psalm 103 at the top of this page do you need to apply today?

- Jesus found the Samaritan woman at the well. Where did he find you? If you have time, share your stories with one another.

Prayer

As you prepare for prayer time, each woman will receive a small piece of paper or a sticky note.

On your note, complete one of these lines:

- Praise God, I have been set free from _____.

- Because of Jesus, my guilt about _____ has been wiped away.

- I am thankful that God's mercy and grace have removed my regret about _____.

If you're willing, please sign your name on your paper. Your leader, or a volunteer from your group will collect these slips of paper to lead a time of prayer, praising God for his unconditional love and forgiveness as she reads each slip aloud.

This is your opportunity to celebrate God's amazing grace and mercy.

At-Home Action

- Contact a friend or a neighbor who needs to hear an encouraging word about unconditional love. Invite her to have coffee and ask her if she has ever felt as if she needed to hide her true self from another woman.

  Let her know you have hard days too, and there are times when you feel inadequate.

Journaling Page

Journaling Page

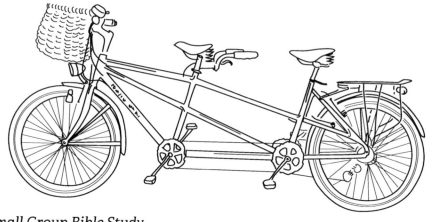

Week Eight: Tenting with Tent Caterpillars

Learning Through Tough Times

Preparation

Please read chapter 8 of *The Repurposed and Upcycled Life.*

Warm Up

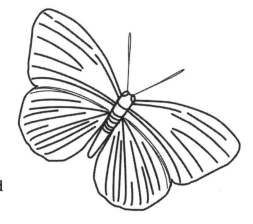

Complete one of the following statements:

- My favorite vacation memory ever is _____.

- My best camping adventure ever was _____.

- The most memorable travel disaster I have ever experienced was _____.

- We made the most of a difficult vacation situation when _____.

Explore the Bible

None of us looks forward to the next difficulty with eager anticipation. We don't expect to do the right thing and have someone turn on us anyway. We don't get up in the morning hoping it will be the day our financial stability flushes away with one flip of the "you're fired" or "we're downsizing" lever. Nor do we plan to have someone start a vicious rumor that destroys our good name.

Those things happen to people every day, though. Life is hard. Sometimes, the difficulty can come even when we're doing everything possible to live a life that honors God.

Read 1 Peter 4:1-19. (Peter wrote this passage as a letter to his fellow Christians, who were going through a difficult time of persecution.)

As you read, look for these concepts:

1. What was happening to the people to whom Peter was writing?

2. Why were they going through this persecution?

Discuss

- 1 Peter 4:4 talks about former friends who are upset with those who are changed because of their new obedience to God. If you have had friends turn their backs on you when you did the right thing, share how that made you feel.

- Read 1 Peter 4:8 again. What do you think it means when it says to show "deep love."

- What do you think it means when it says that love covers a multitude of sins?

1 Peter 4:12-19 specifically addresses persecution for being a Christian. In verse 13, it says to be glad, or rejoice, in these trials.

- What do you think it looks like to "rejoice" in difficulty?

- When you experience something difficult, especially when you are trying to do a good thing, what is your typical reaction when the difficulty comes? You can be honest. Do you retreat? Throw things? Yell? Ask God why? Cry? Sit down and quit?

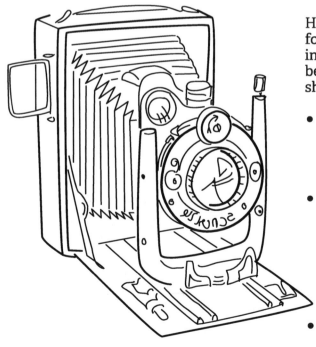

Making Do with Less

Have you ever had to make do in a situation? Perhaps you forgot your makeup on a trip. Or you ran out of a key ingredient for a recipe. Maybe your finances ran short before the next paycheck and you had to adjust for the shortfall.

- Share about how making do taught you something about yourself.

- As you look back at difficulties that you have come through, how can you see now how you grew and learned through the experience, when everything once seemed hopeless in the middle of the situation?

- **Read Philippians 4: 11-12.** Discuss the difference between having all we need versus all we want.

- Often, it isn't our situation that is the true problem, but out attitude toward it. If you could change one thing about your own attitude right now, what would it be?

On the flip side of having the right attitude in tough times, we also need to avoid stuffing our feelings and pretending everything is ok. If there is something you've been pushing through by telling your friends, "I'm fine," if you really aren't, today is the day to be real and open up with your group.

As you move into your prayer time, consider how you might support each other with the knowledge that there is someone walking through this with you.

- Share one thing, big or small, that is going on in your life, and that would be easier to face if you knew others were praying for you.

Prayer

Pray for what you just shared above. If your group is comfortable, break into groups of 2-3 and pray for the others in your huddle. Acknowledge God's power over the situations shared and ask for his presence to be a reminder of hope in each one. Pray for attitude adjustments where needed.

At-Home Action

- Read Luke 12:22-31. Journal about the things you typically worry about. Then, write about what it would look like to "seek the Kingdom of God" above all else. Describe what it means to you to have all you need.

- Read Isaiah 43:1-3. God promises to walk through us in difficulty. He also gave us relationships with others who are walking through life with us. Reach out to someone who you know could use a reminder that someone cares.

"Do not be afraid, for I have ransomed you. I have called you by name; you are mine. When you go through deep waters, When you go through rivers of difficulty, you will not drown. When you walk through the fire of oppression, you will not be burned up; the flames will not consume you. For I am the Lord, your God, the Holy One of Israel, your Savior."

from Isaiah 43:1-3

Journaling Page

_____

_____

_____

_____

_____

_____

_____

_____

_____

_____

_____

_____

_____

_____

_____

_____

_____

_____

_____

_____

_____

_____

Journaling Page

Journaling Page

Week Nine: Only You Can Prevent Frustration Fires
Getting Through Crisis Without Getting Burned

Preparation

Please read chapter 9 of *The Repurposed and Upcycled Life.*

Warm Up

Anger is often a natural response to frustration. Sometimes it comes because our situation feels hopeless, and lashing out feels temporarily good. Other times it is because we feel we have been unfairly treated, or we have experienced injustice.

Whether you work inside the home, or work outside of the home, you have likely had a moment where you felt overwhelmed, under appreciated, and ready to explode with emotion.

- What fuels your frustration? Describe a situation from your life that caused your frustration meter to dial up to a red alert.

Exploring the Bible

God called the prophet Jeremiah to be his messenger to warn the kingdom of Judah of coming destruction and judgment if the people didn't return to God. Of course, this assignment made Jeremiah unpopular with the leaders of Judah. Jeremiah experienced verbal battles with kings, other prophets, priests and leaders.

In addition to the book of Jeremiah, we also have the book of Lamentations, which is almost like having a look inside Jeremiah's journal as he responded to the horror of the destruction that the people experienced because of their refusal to listen to God's message.

Read Lamentations 3:1-33. Note that the author acknowledges how he feels about the experience he has been through.

- List some of of the feelings he conveys in verses 1-19.

- Read verse 20 again. Discuss a time when you grieved over something that you would never forget.

- Even though we don't forget our grief or bitterness, we can discover hope while we process through it. Read verse 21-24. Describe what it means to "hope in the Lord" when everything seems to be crumbling around you.

- Read verse 31. If you have you ever felt as if God had abandoned you, describe that experience.

"I pray that God, the source of hope, will fill you completely with joy and peace because you trust in him. Then you will overflow with confident hope through the power of the Holy Spirit."
Romans 15:13

- What would you say to someone who feels as if God has abandoned them in the middle of their struggle?

- What are some things people say that are not helpful in this type of situation?

Our Hope in His Hands

Hope is confident expectation. When we hope in God, it means we confidently expect that he has a bigger plan than we can see. We confidently expect he will turn things around or change us in some way for the better.

- What thoughts or feelings do you have that can block your hope, or confident expectation, in God?

- What is a healthy way of handling the emotions that block us from having hope?

- What prevents you from running *to* God instead of *from* God when you're in the middle of life's difficulties?

Aligning with Reality

Disappointment is greatest when our expectations don't align with our reality. Life has some curves and ups and downs–that's reality.

- Comparison can lead to foolish choices. It can rob us of joy and peace, and diminish the beauty of God's blessings in our lives. Name some of the blessings you have that you don't notice when you compare yourself to someone else.

- Comparison can go the other way, too. Sometimes we think we are better than someone else. **Read Galatians 6:4-5.** How can we keep our competitive spirit in check?

- **Read 2 Corinthians 12:9-10.** How could weakness, difficulty or trouble be something we take pleasure i n?

- What is your biggest challenge with the idea of embracing difficulty rather than avoiding it?

If we allow a spark of disappointment to grow into a flame and then into a blaze, it can become difficult to manage its destruction. If we can extinguish the thoughts before they take over our lives, we will experience victory!

- What change will you make this week that aligns your heart with God's truth and his purpose for your life?

- What will be your plan of action for when you catch yourself comparing yourself with someone else?

One thing that can cause an alignment problem is when our expectations are connected to comparing ourselves to someone else's reality. It can lead to all sorts of negative thoughts that block us from reaching toward the potential God put within us. Emotions such as: jealousy, disappointment, discouragement, discontentment, hurt or sadness.

Prayer

Pray the words of Psalm 139:1-17, 23-24 for your closing prayer:

You have searched me, Lord, and you know me. You know when I sit and when I rise; you perceive my thoughts from afar. You discern my going out and my lying down; you are familiar with all my ways. Before a word is on my tongue you, Lord, know it completely. You hem me in behind and before, and you lay your hand upon me. Such knowledge is too wonderful for me, too lofty for me to attain. Where can I go from your Spirit? Where can I flee from your presence? If I go up to the heavens, you are there; if I make my bed in the depths, you are there. If I rise on the wings of the dawn, if I settle on the far side of the sea, even there your hand will guide me, your right hand will hold me fast. If I say, "Surely the darkness will hide me and the light become night around me," even the darkness will not be dark to you; the night will shine like the day, for darkness is as light to you. For you created my inmost being; you knit me together in my mother's womb. I praise you because I am fearfully and wonderfully made; your works are wonderful, I know that full well. My frame was not hidden from you when I was made in the secret place, when I was woven together in the depths of the earth. 16 Your eyes saw my unformed body; all the days ordained for me were written in your book before one of them came to be. How precious to me are your thoughts, God! How vast is the sum of them! ...Search me, God, and know my heart; test me and know my anxious thoughts. See if there is any offensive way in me, and lead me in the way everlasting. Amen.

At-Home Activity

Create your own "crisis" kit that you can grab when you feel your frustration level rising. Your kit might include:

- *A small Bible.*
- *A collection of note cards with helpful verses written out on them.*
- *A pen and notebook.*
- *A book of scripture promises or a devotional book.*

You might have other ideas that you could add to your kit. Find a box or a basket to keep these items together in a place where you can easily access them when you're facing a moment when you could use a biblical pep talk.

- Journal about healthy ways you could deal with frustration in your own life:

Journal

_____

_____

_____

_____

_____

_____

_____

_____

_____

_____

_____

Journaling Page

Journaling Page

_____

_____

_____

_____

_____

_____

_____

_____

_____

_____

_____

_____

_____

_____

_____

_____

_____

_____

_____

_____

_____

Week Ten: Blue Light Specials & Bread Bags in My Boots
Rejoicing and Finding Contentment

Preparation

Please read chapter 10 of *The Repurposed and Upcycled Life.*

Warm Up

If you have ever been to a thrift shop or a yard sale, what was your favorite find?

Write your own definition of the word "riches:"

_____

_____

Discuss your definitions as a group.

In this lesson, we are going to explore riches, contentment, God's provision and more. As we explore Scripture, look for ideas that you have about money or possessions that have been formed in part by your childhood culture.

Explore the Bible

Read Matthew 13:1-8, 18-23.

This is one of Jesus' parables. Parables are stories that express an analogy between a common aspect of life and a spiritual truth. In this case, Jesus explained the meaning himself. With other parables, sometimes we're left to speculate about the meaning.

Let's look at the second part of the parable, and then we will come back to the first part of it in a bit.

Discuss

In verse 22, Jesus spoke of the competing demands of life. One of these is worry.

- How has worry, specifically related to finances or possessions, been a distraction for you in life?

- How have possessions, either the lack of, or the surplus of, affected your focus on spiritual things?

This Bible passage connects the lure of wealth (vs. 22) with a crowding out of the message of the gospel. Jesus said no fruit is produced when wealth crowds out the message of God's word.

- What do you think he meant by "no fruit is produced?"

In verse 23, Jesus described what happens when we hear and understand, and the "seed" of God's Word begins to grow.

- As you look back over verses 18-23, describe some of the things you think get in the way of spiritual growth in your own life.

Have you ever noticed that once you have more money, you're hungry for even more? There is only one thing that will really satisfy us: seeking God's kingdom and his way of life. When we do this, other things come second to following Christ, and happiness becomes a byproduct instead of the goal.

Read Colossians 1:9-14.

Let's suppose you set your mind on pursuing Christ and knowing God more, rather than on thinking about the next home or car you plan to buy. In the box below are concepts from the passage you just read. Take a few minutes to have each person in your group write what kind of outcome (fruit) you could expect to see in your life if you gained more of each of these principles.

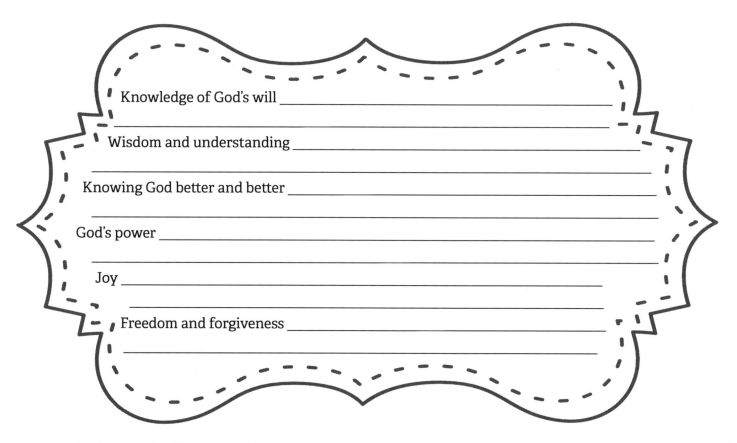

Knowledge of God's will _____

_____

Wisdom and understanding _____

_____

Knowing God better and better _____

_____

God's power _____

_____

Joy _____

_____

Freedom and forgiveness _____

_____

Cornelia "Corrie" ten Boom (1892-1983) was a Dutch watchmaker and Christian who, along with her family members, helped many Jews escape the Nazi Holocaust during World War II by hiding them in their home.

Corrie was imprisoned for her actions and eventually transferred to a concentration camp, where she endured harsh conditions and cruelty. Despite loss and hardship, Corrie pressed on with the mission God placed on her heart.

After the war, she returned to The Netherlands to set up a rehabilitation center for concentration camp survivors and anyone in need of care. She later returned to Germany and met with and forgave two Germans who had been employed at the concentration camp, including one who was particularly cruel to her dear sister Betsie who died while imprisoned.

Corrie went on to travel the world as a public speaker and wrote many books.[1] She once said in an interview, "I've learned that we must hold everything loosely, because when I grip it tightly, it hurts when the Father pries my fingers loose and takes it from me!"[2]

Read Philippians 4:11-13.

- What was Paul's secret for being content, even if he had nothing?

- Money and possessions aren't the only thing in life. Sometimes, our plans aren't God's plans. Discuss how we can still find the blessings when discouragement gets in the way.

If you lost everything, what would you still have? Too often, we seek God's blessings, but we don't seek God.

- What can you do this week that will help you to seek God more? Write down one action step below that you will take to put your focus more on God, and less on worrying about earthly things that have no eternal value:

_____

_____

Prayer

Ask God for a perspective change. Divide up in groups of 2-4 people and share one thing that you're trusting God to change your perspective on. Then pray for each other.

1. Story found in: www.biography.com/people/corrie-ten-boom-21358155
2. Charles Swindoll, *Living Above the Level of Mediocrity*, p.114

At-Home Action

If you're overwhelmed with possessions, or overstretched with bills, consider taking one or more of these steps to release your grip on material things and switch your focus toward God:

- **Discuss.** If you're married, talk about your desire to change your focus with your spouse. Work on a plan of action together.

- **Declutter.** Begin with one closet and see how many things you can donate or toss. When you're ready, continue working through the whole house. Have a garage sale or bring a load to your local thrift store. You may also want to sort your pantry and freezer to begin using up or tossing the excess.

- **Debt.** Put together a strategy for getting out of debt. There are many programs that can help. One place where you can find practical resources to help is from personal finance teacher, Joe Sangl. **www.josephsangl.com**

- **Deactivate.** Along with the previous step, if store credit cards and loyalty programs tempt you too much, why not deactivate or destroy all but the ones you need?

- **Downsize.** It's a bigger step than some of the others, but consider if your home or cars are more than what you need.

life on two wheels

Journaling Page

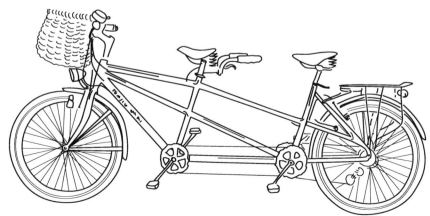

Journaling Page

_____

_____

_____

_____

_____

_____

_____

_____

_____

_____

_____

_____

_____

_____

_____

_____

_____

_____

_____

_____

_____

_____

_____

_____

Week Eleven: Please Hold, an Operator Will Assist You Shortly
Connecting with God in Prayer

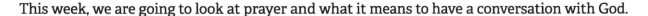

Preparation

Please read chapter 11 of *The Repurposed and Upcycled Life*.

Warm Up

- Describe how you feel when you think someone isn't really listening to you.

- How do you feel when a conversation seems to be one-sided?

Perhaps you have had a difficult conversation with customer service, similar to the one described in the book. Thank goodness, God doesn't put us on hold while he consults his boss - he *is* the boss! And we aren't customers; we are his children.

This week, we are going to look at prayer and what it means to have a conversation with God.

Explore the Bible

Let's explore the story of Hannah, a woman from the Bible. Hannah was one of two women who were married to Elkanah. Although having two wives was a common practice in the Old Testament, it hardly came without trouble! As might be expected, here was some conflict between Peninnah and Hannah.

Read 1 Samuel 1:1-20.

It wasn't just that Hannah wasn't able conceive a child. To make it worse, Peninnah—let's call her Penny—taunted Hannah about it.

Discuss

- Describe how you would feel if you were in Hannah's shoes.

- Discuss how it feels to want something so badly, but when you pray about it, God doesn't answer in the way you'd hoped.

Read what Elkanah said in verse 8.

• How do you feel when you long for something, but someone says to you, "At least you have _____..."

• This passage describes Hannah's prayer as pouring her heart out to the Lord. Describe a time, past or present, when you have poured your heart out to the Lord.

• What does it feel like if it seems as if he doesn't hear, or isn't listening when you cry out to God?

In verse 16, Hannah told Eli, the priest, she was praying out of great anguish and sorrow. Eli didn't understand her actions at first, and even thought her to be a crazy woman. But once he understood her heart, he encouraged her and offered a blessing.

• If there has been a time in your life when someone encouraged you to believe that God hears your prayers, share about how that helped you.

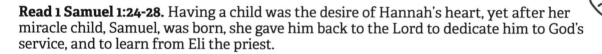

Read 1 Samuel 1:24-28. Having a child was the desire of Hannah's heart, yet after her miracle child, Samuel, was born, she gave him back to the Lord to dedicate him to God's service, and to learn from Eli the priest.

• Share about a time when you released something to God that was precious to you. How did you feel?

Read Hannah's prayer of praise in **1 Samuel 2:1-11**. This is her testimony of being vindicated when God heard her prayer and responded. She said, "My heart rejoices in the Lord."

• Discuss the difference between rejoicing in the Lord, versus rejoicing in our circumstances.

• How does rejoicing in the Lord help us to cope if he has a different answer for our prayers than what we would like?

  *Created for Relationship*

God created you to have a relationship with him. Like a dear friend, he is there for you to pour out your heart, just as Hannah did. Prayer offers comfort when we give God our disappointment and broken hearts.

2 Corinthians 1:3-4 says, "All praise to God, the Father of our Lord Jesus Christ. God is our merciful Father and the source of all comfort. He comforts us in all our troubles so that we can comfort others. When they are troubled, we will be able to give them the same comfort God has given us."

- Share with your group what you will pour out to God in prayer this week.

Plan for Connection

If you have been encouraged, who will you comfort in their time of trouble? Make a plan to call or check in with someone who needs a blessing this week.

Prayer

There are many places in the Bible where laying hands on someone was part of prayer. Whether it was for a prayer of blessing, for healing, for setting apart in service or conveying wisdom or strength, placing your hands on the person for whom you're praying can be a meaningful prayer experience.

Select a chair to be the "hot seat" and take turns praying for each person in the group who would like to participate. Gather around the person and place a hand on her shoulder or head as a few people in your group pray.

At-Home Action

Prayer is really just a conversation with God; it's like talking with a friend, only more powerful than you can imagine! Set aside specific time to T.A.L.K. with God. As you pray, practice these actions: Thank, Ask, Listen, Know.

Thank – Gratitude is a way of worshiping God. Thank God for who he is and for what he has done. Include praise with your worship to God.

Ask – Yes, God knows what you need, but he wants you to ask him. Ask him to answer according to his will, what he knows is best for us. Ask for forgiveness as you confess wrongs you have done.

Listen – Leave space in your prayer time to listen quietly. Instead of doing all of the talking, see what God speaks to your heart. Be comfortable just being with him, rather than doing.

Know – Like an intimate conversation, prayer helps us to know God more, and in knowing him more, we know his love, his will and his heart. Knowing him through prayer builds our faith for when testing comes. It also helps us create a habit of talking to him like a friend throughout the day.

Journaling Page

_____

_____

_____

_____

_____

_____

_____

_____

_____

_____

_____

_____

_____

_____

_____

_____

_____

_____

_____

_____

_____

_____

_____

_____

Journaling Page

Journaling Page

_____
_____
_____
_____
_____
_____
_____
_____
_____
_____
_____
_____
_____
_____
_____
_____
_____
_____
_____
_____
_____
_____
_____
_____

Week Twelve: Girl*fiend* or a Girlfriend?

Enjoying Real Friendship with Women

Preparation

Please read chapter 12 of *The Repurposed and Upcycled Life*.

Warm Up

In a culture of social media and digital connections, we have many people call friends, but it is uncommon to have deep, real friendships. Those connections with people who "get" us, hold us accountable, support us when we need it and who need us just as much, are precious and rare. Friends can be the ones who helps us learn how to live like Jesus and soften our rough edges.

- Who has been your friend for the longest of all?

- What is it about your friendship with this person that you think has made it last this long?

Explore the Bible

One of the books of the Bible that has a lot to say about friendship is the book of Proverbs. As we explore what God's word says, we are going to look at it in the context of R.E.A.L. friendships, as presented in The Repurposed and Upcycled Life.

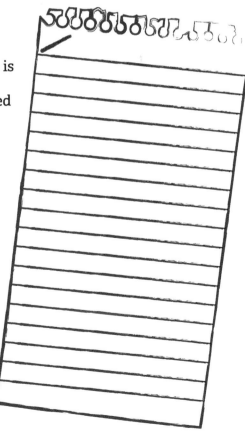

    R.E.A.L. friends:

        *R*emember you need each other

        *E*ncourage one another

        *A*ccept each other unconditionally

        *L*ove sacrificially

Read Proverbs 27:1-11.

- In the graphic to the right, list some of the principles of friendship that stand out to you from this passage.

Discuss

Let's discuss some of the specifics we find in Proverbs that connect with R.E.A.L. friendship. The questions following each Proverb will help you apply the concept to everyday life.

Remember you need each other
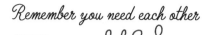

The godly give good advice to their friends; the wicked lead them astray. —Proverbs 12:26

• How do you think you can tell if a friend is giving good advice or bad advice?

Many will say they are loyal friends, but who can find one who is truly reliable? —Proverbs 20:6

• Describe what it means to you to have a friend who is loyal and reliable.

As iron sharpens iron, so a friend sharpens a friend. —Proverbs 27:17

• Sometimes the best interactions with a friend are the ones that are a little more difficult to embrace. How has a friend's healthy criticism or accountability helped you to become a better person?

Encourage one another

A troublemaker plants seeds of strife; gossip separates the best of friends. —Proverbs 16:28

• How do you feel when you find out someone who you thought was a friend has talked about you behind your back.

• How can you make a personal commitment to make sure your friends know they can trust you?

The heartfelt counsel of a friend is as sweet as perfume and incense. —Proverbs 27:9

• When a friend gives you advice, how do you know it is heartfelt?

• How can you encourage friends without it seeming as if you are trying to fix them?

Accept each other unconditionally

An open rebuke is better than hidden love! Wounds from a sincere friend are better than many kisses from an enemy. —Proverbs 27:5-6

- If a friend truly loves you, she will have your best interest at heart. When you have to speak difficult words to a friend, how can you be sure to present them in a way that she understands that you love her unconditionally?

Don't befriend angry people or associate with hot-tempered people, or you will learn to be like them and endanger your soul. —Proverbs 22:24–25

- If someone who you think is a true friend, but she's easily upset and you have to tiptoe around her feelings often, that can be a challenge. It might even mean you need to part ways. How can you love someone unconditionally, but still maintain healthy boundaries when you realize your friendship isn't healthy?

Love sacrificially

There are "friends" who destroy each other, but a real friend sticks closer than a brother. —Proverbs 18:24

- What is the most heart-touching sacrifice a friend has ever made for you?

A friend is always loyal, and a brother is born to help in time of need. —Proverbs 17:17

- Sometimes friends are actually closer to us than family. Read what Jesus said in **John 15:9-14.** How does the love friends have for one another connect with the love Jesus has for each of us?

My child, never forget the things I have taught you. Store my commands in your heart. If you do this, you will live many years, and your life will be satisfying. Never let loyalty and kindness leave you! Tie them around your neck as a reminder. Write them deep within your heart. Then you will find favor with both God and people, and you will earn a good reputation. —Proverbs 3:1-4

- What are some ways you can work on being a good friend, rather than seeking to find good friends?

- As you think about your own attitudes toward friends, how can you make sure you remain other-centered rather than self-centered in your relationships?

Prayer

Pair up and pray for each other using these paraphrased Bible passages as a blessing. Fill in a specific name in the blank as you pray and then switch.

I pray that from his glorious, unlimited resources God will empower _____ with inner strength through his Spirit. Then Christ will make his home in her heart as she trusts in him. May _____'s roots grow down into God's love and keep her strong. And may she have the power to understand, as all God's people should, how wide, how long, how high, and how deep his love is. May she experience the love of Christ, though it is too great to understand fully. Then she will be made complete with all the fullness of life and power that comes from God. (Based on Ephesians 3:16-19).

May the Lord bless and protect _____. May the Lord smile on her and be gracious to her. May the Lord show _____ his favor and give her his peace. Amen. (Based on Numbers 6:24-26).

At-Home Action

Practice being a R.E.A.L. friend with these challenges:

Remember you need each other
- How can you be intentional in your friendships? Reach out to a friend who you haven't contacted in a while. Whether it is a phone call, email, handwritten note, or an online chat, invest in finding out how she has been doing.

Encourage one another
- Send a note to a friend to remind her you're there for her, to congratulate her for a recent accomplishment, or to let her know you care.

Accept each other unconditionally
- If you have had a misunderstanding with a friend, approach her to make amends.

Love sacrificially
- Friendships will cost you something: time, energy, comfort, and even yourself. What are you willing to set aside for a friend who could use your support right now?
- What will your next step be in taking action?

Journaling Page

Journaling Page

_____

_____

_____

_____

_____

_____

_____

_____

_____

_____

_____

_____

_____

_____

_____

_____

_____

_____

_____

_____

_____

_____

Week Thirteen: Three Little Pigs and the Proverbs 31 Woman

Being the Best Woman You Can Be, Realistically

Preparation

Please read chapter 13 of *The Repurposed and Upcycled Life.*

Warm Up

- Who is a female role model that you look up to?

- What is it about her that you admire?

- If you're familiar with Proverbs 31, what comes to mind when you hear someone mention "the Proverbs 31 woman?"

Explore the Bible

Read Proverbs 31:10-31 together. This section was written as an acrostic poem in Hebrew, with each verse beginning with a latter of the Hebrew alphabet.

- Now that you have read the passage, what thoughts come to mind that you didn't already discuss?

- As you look through the qualities described here, which ones seem most achievable, and which seem out of reach for you?

Discuss

Sometimes, when we read passages like this, we see a picture of perfection or a standard that we aren't sure we can live up to in our everyday life. Let's set Proverbs aside for a moment and look at our culture and our expectations.

- If you're on social media such as Facebook or Instagram, or something similar, what role does artificial perfection play in how you view yourself as a woman, wife, or mother?

- Perhaps as you read about the woman in Proverbs 31 you thought she would be more aptly named the Pinterest Woman. What danger is there in setting our own bar as high as what we see presented in the projects, clothing, homemaking, and such on Pinterest?

- How does comparison with other women lead to a flawed motive?

Read 1 Peter 1:13-16.

- Rather than pursuing perfection, or a worldly standard, what does God want us to pursue?

- The poem in Proverbs 31 was most likely written for an audience of men as a piece to honor the value of a godly woman. Discuss how the type of woman described in the poem provides an example of pursuing godliness and holiness, rather than perfection.

- Let's discuss some of the qualities represented in Proverbs 31. As you discuss each of these, share how these can be done with the motive of pleasing God, rather than people.
    o Working hard
    o Resourcefulness
    o Thrifty and frugal
    o Wise with finances
    o Prepared for all seasons
    o Practical
    o Honorable
    o Strong and dignified
    o Wise with words
    o Kind
    o Fears the Lord

- What other qualities do you see here? How might those same concepts be represented in a modern woman, one who doesn't buy a field or plant a vineyard?

When we do our best and strive for excellence rather than perfection, it is God we seek to please, rather than people. But what happens when life gets really hard and we don't see an immediate reward for our labor? What about when no one seems to appreciate what we do?

- Discuss what encouragement you can offer to a woman who feels undervalued and under-appreciated for all she does.

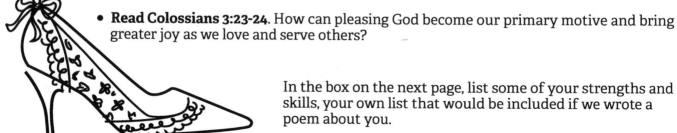

- **Read Colossians 3:23-24.** How can pleasing God become our primary motive and bring greater joy as we love and serve others?

In the box on the next page, list some of your strengths and skills, your own list that would be included if we wrote a poem about you.

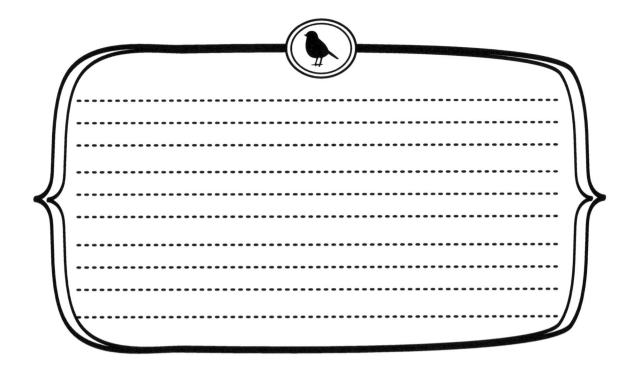

Make a Connection

Before you close, have each person share one thing about someone else in the group that you see as a quality that is honoring to God in the same way as the qualities represented in Proverbs 31.

Prayer

As you begin prayer time, go around the room and share one of your strengths and one thing that you want God to work on changing in you. Then take turns praying for one another.

Choose one accountability person to check in with during the week. Before you leave, take time to each make a note of your prayer requests. When you check in by phone, email or social media this week, make a point of asking about that specific need.

At-Home Action

Read Galatians 1:10 and ask yourself who you're really striving to please. Journal about your thoughts in relation to that verse.

Do you play the comparison game? It can lead to several outcomes, including:

- Despair – feeling discouraged, as if you'll never measure up
- Envy – disliking other women who you perceive to have something you don't have
- Pride – thinking, "at least I'm not as bad as so-and-so."

Again, work through your thoughts in your journal if you're experiencing any of the three things listed above. Ask God to change your motive and help you stop playing comparison games. Receive the grace he offers for your struggle.

Journaling Page

Journaling Page

Journaling Page

_____

_____

_____

_____

_____

_____

_____

_____

_____

_____

_____

_____

_____

_____

_____

_____

_____

_____

_____

_____

_____

_____

_____

_____

_____

Week Fourteen: Zzz...Yawning or Yearning?

Rekindling a Passion for God

Preparation

Please read chapter 14 of *The Repurposed and Upcycled Life*.

Warm Up

Are you a sleepwalker? A sleep-talker? Maybe you have crazy dreams that you remember when you wake up.

- What is the craziest thing you have ever done when you were sleeping?

- Or what is the most outrageous dream you can remember?

As you think back over your life, have there been times when you were more excited about spiritual things than other times? Maybe you're in one of those seasons right now where you're on fire for your faith. Or maybe you feel like you've been hitting the snooze for a while and you're not fully awake spiritually at this time. In some seasons, people feel as if they are in a spiritual fog. This group is a safe place for you, wherever you're at in your journey!

- Which would you say best describes you right now?

    a) I feel more spiritually awake and alive right now than ever before!

    b) I feel like I'm making a turnaround after having been sort of apathetic for a while. I'm ready to take a new step.

    c) I wish I could recapture what I had at one time, but I'm feeling stuck. I'm not quite sure what to do next.

    d) I feel far from God right now, and I could use some friends who accept me while I question.

Explore the Bible

Read Ephesians 2:1-10. In this letter, Paul writes to the people at Ephesus who are followers of Christ. He reminds them of the good news of God's grace in Jesus Christ, and emphasizes that it is for all who believe, both Jews and Gentiles. Then he explains some guidelines for how to live as believers in Jesus.

- In the beginning of this chapter, Paul reminds his readers that they were once like dead people before God. Discuss what you think it means to be spiritually dead.

- Our bodies will die someday, but what does it mean in verse 6 when it says that God raised us from the dead when he raised Jesus from the dead?

- What does being "raised from the dead" mean for us while we live here on earth?

- What does it mean for us in the future after our physical body dies?

Discuss

One of the best ways to discover our passion is to discover our purpose. And one of the best ways to discover our purpose is to get our hearts aligned with God through worship.

Read Psalm 51:10-13. King David wrote this after he had committed a great sin, and he was asking God for forgiveness.

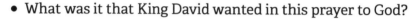

- What was it that King David wanted in this prayer to God?

- What purpose did he see for his life, even in the midst of the fallout of his sin?

David often worshipped God when he was experiencing difficult times. Worship changes our focus and reminds us that our purpose in life isn't about us. It shifts our focus from our problem, to the problem solver.

Passion and Purpose

We all have a unique purpose where God will use our gift and talents, but we also have a common purpose: love. Jesus often emphasized the importance of love.

Read Luke 10:25-28.

Here, one of the experts in the religious law wanted to trap Jesus, but instead Jesus asked him to summarize the core of the law. Essentially, it is these two things: *Love God. Love people.*

- Discuss what it means to love God with all of your heart, soul, strength and mind.

- What are some practical ways you can love God with your thoughts and emotions?

- How can you love him with all of your body and actions?

- What does it mean to "love your neighbor?"

Awakening Your Passion

In groups of 2-3 women, discuss the following questions:

- What has someone else told you that you were good at?

- If you aren't already using the gifts God has given you to love God and love people, what is holding you back right now?

- If you took one step of action to pursue passion and purpose, what step would you take this week?

Prayer

Stay in your groups of 2-3 and pray together about what you just discussed. Pray God would release the lies that have bound you and kept you from loving him and loving people with all of your heart. Pray for boldness in leaving behind the past and moving forward with God's direction.

At-Home Action

Schedule some time soon to take a day, an afternoon or a weekend for personal reflection (You may want to wait until after next week's lesson and combine this with that activity). If you stay home, find a quiet place where you feel at peace and you can think. Perhaps you'll go to the park for an afternoon, or go to a bed and breakfast for a weekend. Maybe you'll borrow a friend's cabin at the lake.

As you have your personal retreat, ask yourself these questions and write in your journal:

- Am I satisfied with my passion for God and my relationship with him? If not, where would I like that passion to be?

- What needs to change so that he becomes my focus in life?

- How do I want people to remember me?

- What would others say I am most passionate about?

- How has God gifted me?

- Am I surrounded more by people and situations that wake me up spiritually, or make me more spiritually asleep?

- What changes do I need to make about those influences?

If you would like to learn more about your spritiaul gifts, this website is a great place ot start:
www.spiritualgiftstest.com

Journaling Page

_____

_____

_____

_____

_____

_____

_____

_____

_____

_____

_____

_____

_____

_____

_____

_____

_____

_____

_____

_____

_____

_____

Journaling Page

Journaling Page

_____
_____
_____
_____
_____
_____
_____
_____
_____
_____
_____
_____
_____
_____
_____
_____
_____
_____
_____
_____
_____
_____
_____
_____
_____
_____

Week Fifteen: Chicken Coop for the Soul
Daring to Dream of God's Purpose

Preparation

Please read chapter 15 of *The Repurposed and Upcycled Life.*

Warm Up

This week, we are going to wrap up everything we have studied over the past weeks. As you think about living a repurposed and upcycled life, you can be sure God has something uniquely designed for you to fulfill his purpose for you.

> Fill in the blank and share with the group: If I could do something meaningful in life, my dream is to_____.

A repurposed and upcycled life is really about living with no regrets. It's living in God's grace, free of the past, and stepping forward to bring glory to God.

You were made for something more than a chicken coop! Last week, we talked about your passion and purpose. This week, we will talk about your dream. God has placed a dream in your heart that is uniquely tailored for you.

- Why do you think many people are afraid to tell other people about their dream?

- What do you think is the difference between a dream and a calling? Do you think they can they be the same thing? Why or why not?

Explore the Bible

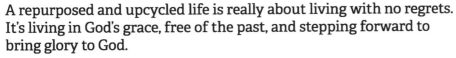

Read Isaiah 40:25-31.

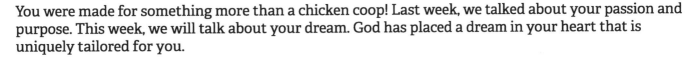

This is part of a message that the prophet Isaiah brought to the Israelite people to remind them of God's character and his purpose for Israel. Even though our purpose is different from that of the Israelites, the principles of this message can still apply to us personally. Like these people so long ago, we need the reminder that God is merciful, that he can rescue us, and that he is powerful enough to handle our struggles.

- This passage begins with, "Look up into the heavens..." As you look into the sky, what does the universe tell you about the God who created it, and who created you?

- The God of the universe cares about every one of us and our hopes, dreams, and purpose. What does that mean for you personally when you stop to think about it?

Discuss

- In Isaiah 40: 29, it says God gives power to the weak and strength to the powerless. What does this mean for you as you think about your dream?

- Verse 31 talks about those who trust in the Lord. Some versions say, "those who wait on the Lord." What is the difference between waiting on the Lord and procrastinating when it comes to your dream?

Chickens have feathers and wings, and all of the equipment to fly, but they are content to stay in the coop. Eagles are powerful birds that fly far and high.

- What does God promise when we trust in him?

Read 2 Timothy 1:6-7

- What does the Spirit of God give us and how do these apply to living out the dream God has given you?

Facing Obstacles

There are several reasons for why we might be more like chickens than eagles in how we live our dreams. As you look at each of these barriers to action, look up and read the verse next to it and then discuss each question.

- **Fear** – Joshua 1:9. Based on what God told Joshua when he gave him a big assignment, what can you assume about what God has assigned to you?

- **Doubt** – Exodus 3:9-12, 4:10-13. When God gave Moses a task to do, Moses had many doubts. What was God's response to his doubt?

- **Complacency** – Colossians 3:23-24. Sometimes, we are happy to pretend that God's promises are for other people. How can this verse be a source of motivation instead of procrastination?

- **Comfort** – James 1:2-4. Our comfort zone can be a place where we make no progress. Why do you think it sometimes is in the times of difficulty where we take action?

- **Naysayers** – Proverbs 12:25. Sometimes, even well-meaning people can be discouraging. What are you afraid people might say if you tell them your dream?

- **Self-limiting beliefs** – Philippians 4:13. A limiting belief is a statement you tell yourself that says "I can't" whenever you think about pursuing a dream God has given you. Name one of your own self-limiting beliefs and then debunk the lie by stating the truth.

    Example: I have too much to do to focus on my dream. The truth is that I will make time for what is really important.

Wrapping Up

Over the past weeks, we have talked about letting go of baggage, living in the freedom of God's grace, getting a healthy perspective on troubles, releasing perfectionism, learning from difficult situations, being a woman of God and finding our passion and purpose.

- As you think about everything we have studied in this small group Bible study, what stands out for you that you have already started to apply to your life?

- Share with the group about one change you have made.

- Share a goal or an action step that you will take next.

Who in your group will be your accountability buddy as you work on that next step? _____ Before you leave today, make a plan to call each other or get together within the next two weeks.

Prayer

As a benediction to wrap up your time together, have someone pray the following prayer, adapted from Ephesians 3:14-21:

> When we think of all this, we fall to our knees and pray to the Father, the Creator of everything in heaven and on earth. We pray that from his glorious, unlimited resources he will empower each of us with inner strength through his Spirit. Then Christ will make his home in our hearts as we trust in him. Our roots will grow down into God's love and keep us strong. And may we have the power to understand, as all God's people should, how wide, how long, how high, and how deep his love is. May we each experience the love of Christ, though it is too great to understand fully. Then we will be made complete with all the fullness of life and power that comes from God. Now all glory to God, who is able, through his mighty power at work within us, to accomplish infinitely more than we might ask or think. Glory to him in the church and in Christ Jesus through all generations forever and ever! Amen.

At-Home Action

As you think about the dream God has called you to, consider the steps that you will need to take in order to be obedient to that call. Write out five to ten "I will" statements that indicate what you will do as a result of this study. Examples: I will put God first by _____, I will use my gifts to _____, I will believe the truth of what God's word says about me...

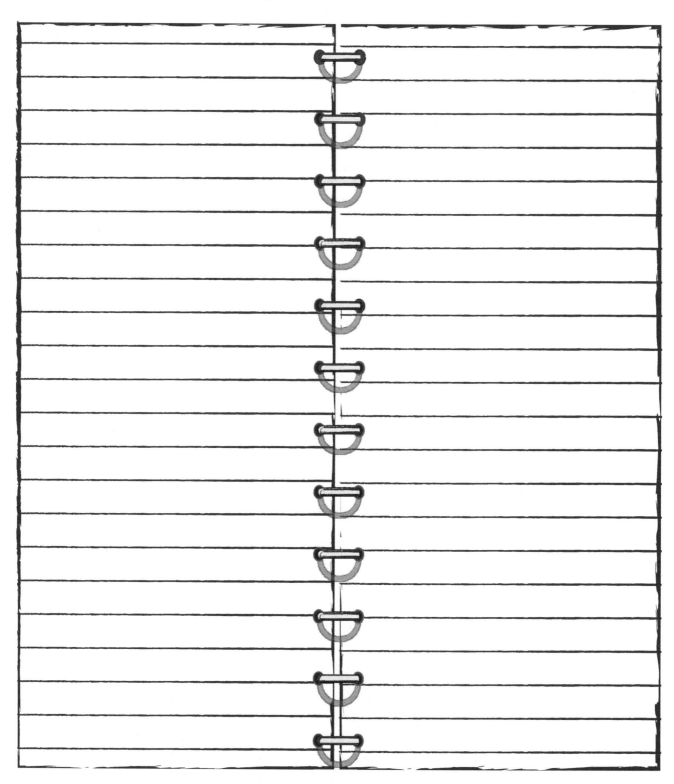

Journaling Page

Journaling Page

_____
_____
_____
_____
_____
_____
_____
_____
_____
_____
_____
_____
_____
_____
_____
_____
_____
_____
_____
_____
_____
_____
_____

Journaling Page

Journaling Page

_____

_____

_____

_____

_____

_____

_____

_____

_____

_____

_____

_____

_____

_____

_____

_____

_____

_____

_____

_____

_____

_____

_____

_____

Journaling Page

Journaling Page

Journaling Page

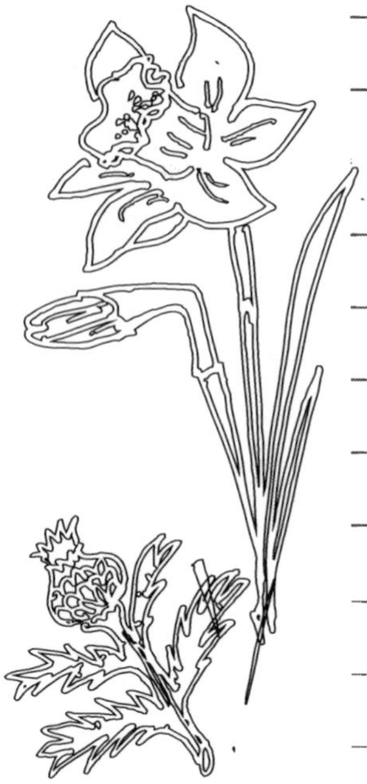

_____

_____

_____

_____

_____

_____

_____

_____

_____

_____

_____

_____

_____

_____

_____

_____

_____

_____

_____

_____

_____

_____

_____

_____

_____

_____

Journaling Page

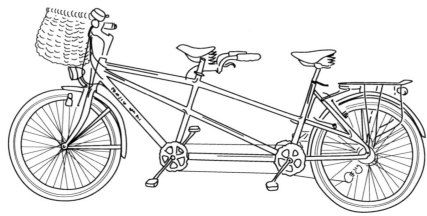

Journaling Page

_____
_____
_____
_____
_____
_____
_____
_____
_____
_____
_____
_____
_____
_____
_____
_____
_____
_____
_____
_____
_____
_____
_____
_____

Leader Notes

Ideas for Leaders

Prepare the meeting space so that it will enhance the learning process. Ideally, group members should be seated in a circle so that all can see one another. Maybe this is around a table, in a living room, or at a cluster of tables at a coffee shop.

- Have a couple of Bibles for those who forget to bring their own. Or encourage participants to download a Bible app to a phone or tablet. Being able to use different translations is helpful.
- Encourage participants to bring journals along with their Bibles book.   , or to use the pages in the
- Have paper and pens or pencils available. For those who want to color in the doodles on the pages, markers or colored pencils will make it fun.

Tips

- Begin and end on time – whatever time you have established.
- Create a climate of openness, encouraging group members to participate as they feel comfortable.
- Give everyone a chance to talk, but keep the conversation moving. Intervene where needed to prevent a few individuals from doing all the talking.
- Model openness as you share with the group. Group members will follow your example. If you take your own sharing below the surface level, others will follow suit.
- Encourage multiple answers or responses before moving on. Take your time with each question.
- Ask, "Why?" or "Can you say more about that?" to help continue a discussion and give it greater depth.
- Ask open-ended questions that cannot be answered with a simple yes or a no. Instead, encourage more thoughtful answers.
- Remember that you do not have all the answers. Your job is to keep the discussion going and encourage participation.
- Stay grounded in the Word of God. If someone says something that doesn't align with the Bible, take an approach of, "Let's see what God's Word says about that."
- Stress confidentiality in your group and remind participants that what is discussed at the group stays with the group.
- Get to know group members by trying to connect for one-on-one time outside of the group at least once during this study. If your group is large, enlist the support of several co-leaders who can do one-on-ones with others.
- Make it fun! This is about building relationships that lead to spiritual growth.

About the Author

Michelle wants to help readers connect the dots between faith, creativity, and everyday life and discover the joy of finding God in the most unexpected places. Years ago, she left her career as a registered nurse to raise her family, and along the way, she discovered her true passion for writing, speaking, and all things creative. Now she works from her home office as a full-time freelance writer, editor and speaker. She has a Master of Arts in ministry leadership with a pastoral counseling emphasis, and she loves ministering to groups of women.

She enjoys repurposing thrift sale finds into fun decorations for her home and garden, mostly because the before and after reminds her of how life goes sometimes. It's in the beauty of restoration and renewal in the midst of disappointing circumstances that she's discovered the most joy in her own life. She blogs about before and after projects and devotional thoughts from life.

Michelle has written many articles for publication, and *The Repurposed and Upcycled Life* was her first book. Her writing has appeared in the *Christian Communicator, Focus on the Family, Chicken Soup for the Soul, Vista, Queen of the Castle Magazine, Today's Christian Living* and more. She has also written several Bible studies for ChristianBibleStudies.com. She is a small group leader at her church and writes a weekly Bible study and discussion guide for all of the small groups to use.

Michelle has been married to her high school sweetheart, Phil, for 28 years and they have two grown sons. They live in an unusual home that was formerly a little country church with a parsonage attached. The church half of it is one hundred years old, and the rest is gradually coming out of the dreadful 50s and 70s decor with ongoing updates and renovation. Michelle has filled their home with creative makeovers of junk treasures.

To connect with Michelle or learn more about having her speak for your event, visit her website at:

www.michellerayburn.com

Email: michelle@michellerayburn.com

Facebook: facebook.com/Michelle.Rayburn.Author

Twitter: twitter.com/michellerayburn

Pinterest: pinterest.com/michellerayburn

87493602R00061

Made in the USA
Lexington, KY
25 April 2018